Shalom Chaveirim

by Robert A. Amchin

A Celebration of Jewish and Hebrew Music
for Voices and Orff Ensemble

With original drawings by Robin Reikes

SMC 575

SCHOTT

Mainz • London • Madrid • New York • Paris • Prague • Tokyo • Toronto

to Deb, Shirin, Benjamin, and Miriam

SMC 575

ISMN 979-0-60001-070-7
UPC   8-41886-01830-3
ISBN 978-1-84761-273-1

Design, typesetting and music engraving by William Holab

Contents

INTRODUCTION

Shalom Chaveirim proclaims "Hello, friends." This collection of elemental arrangements of songs, canons, and dance melodies from the Jewish tradition is offered as a companion to Miriam Samuelson's *Kukuriku* (SMC 57). While most of the selections in this collection contain Hebrew texts because of their Israeli origins, the collection also offers three Nigunim (traditional Yiddish melodies without words) as examples of Jewish music from Eastern Europe. Also included are Hebrew canons with elemental accompaniment. These settings are examples of the cultural heritage of Jews throughout the world. Each selection includes an elemental orchestration, translation or transliteration, and teaching suggestions.

ACKNOWLEDGEMENTS

I have sung the songs in this supplement to the American Orff Schulwerk all my life and have taught them throughout my professional career. It has been a lifelong dream to put them into a collection and share them, and I am so pleased that Schott gave me this opportunity.

Many people helped to make this book a reality. I am grateful to all of the friends, students and colleagues who have played through these arrangements and made suggestions and improvements over the years. Thanks to Robin Reikes for her beautiful artwork. This collection would not have been possible without Carolee Stewart's enthusiastic support and patience. I can't thank her enough for her editorial vision and more importantly for her friendship throughout my career. She and fellow editor Wendy Lampa were instrumental in the completion of this project. Their suggestions, editorial expertise, and support were invaluable.

My sincere thanks also go to Miriam Samuelson who inspired me as a teacher and *mensch*. She was the role model who helped me to explore my own heritage and musicianship from the beginning of my teaching career and ultimately to the creation of this musical celebration. This set of arrangements is intended to be a companion to her collection of songs and dances from the Jewish tradition.

It is a blessing to have a supportive family. Thank you to my children, Shirin, Benjamin and Miriam, who support me in all I do and especially for their input, review of manuscripts, and suggestions while making this book a reality. Most importantly, I could not have completed this project without the loving support and assistance from my wife, Deb.

HEBREW PRONUNCIATION GUIDE

Vowels

a as in f*a*ther or c*a*r
ai as in *ai*sle or s*igh*
e short e as in b*e*d or f*e*d
ei as in *ei*ght or th*ey*
i as in p*i*zza or m*e*
o long o as in g*o* or sl*ow*
u as in l*u*nar or yo*u*
' is an unstressed vowel schwa ə, an unstressed e
oi as in b*o*y

Consonants

ch as in the German Ba*ch* or the Scottish Lo*ch*
g hard g as in *g*et or *g*ive
tz as in boa*ts*
h after a vowel is silent

INSTRUMENTS AND ABBREVIATIONS

V	Voice
SR	Soprano Recorder
SG	Soprano Glockenspiel
AG	Alto Glockenspiel
SX	Soprano Xylophone
AX	Alto Xylophone
BX	Bass Xylophone
SM	Soprano Metallophone
AM	Alto Metallophone
BM	Bass Metallophone
FC	Finger Cymbals
Tr.	Triangle
Cym.	Cymbal
WB	Wood Block
TB	Temple Blocks
Tamb.	Tambourine
HD	Hand Drum
Dr.	Drum

Artzah Alinu

Traditional/Israeli
Text: Sh. Navon

אַרְצָה עָלִינוּ, כְּבָר חָרַשְׁנוּ וְגַם זָרַעְנוּ
אֲבָל עוֹד לֹא קָצַרְנוּ

Artzah Alinu—Teaching Suggestions

About the text

The text declares, "We have gone up to the land of Israel. We have already plowed and sown, but we have not yet harvested." This song can be sung any time of the year. This melody lends itself to movement accompaniment and joyous singing.

About the arrangement

The teacher can introduce the song through echoed imitation. The first half of the song is very repetitive. For the second section of the song, echo the text first without the melody.

The text of this melody may be difficult for singers, though the melody's energetic rhythm will appeal to students. When learning the Hebrew, students might notice the repetition in the text.

> *K'var charashnu v'gam zaranu,* (2 times)
> *Aval od lo katzarnu.* (3 times)

Explore barred percussion parts beginning with the bass xylophone, which is a set of three simple bordun accompaniments with slight pitch changes in the final phrase. Students might use body percussion to outline the arpeggiated and chord bordun patterns and then transfer their sound gestures to barred percussion.

Explore and develop the other parts that complement the phrases of the song. Unpitched parts may be simplified or improvised, based on student ideas. In the hand drum part, notes with stems down imply an accented down stroke. Notes with stems up are unaccented up strokes.

David Melech—Teaching suggestions

About the text
The text of this children's singing game is, "David, king of Israel, lives forever." The name David is pronounced *Dah-veed* in Hebrew. This melody is sung throughout the year as a hand clapping game.

About the arrangement
To begin, the song might be taught through echoed imitation. While teaching the song, students can be introduced to the hand clapping game, as follows [all gestures are eighth notes]:

- Patsch patsch (pat pat)
- Clap clap
- Wave hands over one another (2 beats right over left, then switch)
- Fist bumps one over the other (2 beats right over left, then switch)
- Wave hello with the left hand, and with the right hand to the left elbow for 2 beats, then switch

Repeat the sequence.

(Note: this hand pattern can be seen in the song "Hand Jive" from the film *Grease* as well as in other children's songs.)

The accompaniment is an example of the many two-measure patterns that can be used with this song. Simplify or adjust the patterns based on the skill and experience of the students or sing *a cappella*. Traditionally, children challenge one another to see who can sing while doing the hand motions the fastest.

David Melech

Music: Nachum Frankel
Text: Rosh Hashanah 25a

דָּוִד מֶלֶךְ יִשְׂרָאֵל חַי וְקַיָּם

Lakova Sheli—Teaching suggestions

About the text

The text of this singing game is, "My hat has three corners, three corners has my hat; if it didn't have three corners, it would not be my hat." A fun singing game, it can be performed at any time of the year.

About the arrangement

The teacher might present the song to children through echoed imitation, presenting the Hebrew words to children as it is taught.

The accompaniment consists of a two-measure ostinato outlining the harmony of the song. This might be introduced through echoed or mirrored imitation. The temple block part is only a suggestion and can be adapted to the abilities and experience of the children performing the piece.

The song is best known as an elimination game. For each word, the child points to a particular element of the song, as follows:

- *Lakova sheli* ("my hat [it has]"—point to head)
- *Shalosh* ("three"—hold up three fingers)
- *Pinot* ("corners"—point to bent elbow)
- *V'im lo hayu lo* ("if it did not have"—shake finger "no")
- *Lo haya zeh* ("it would not be"—shake finger "no")
- *Hakova sheli* ("the hat that belongs to me/my hat"—point to head)

With each repetition of the song, part of the text is taken away, as in "Bingo," until only the motions are being performed in pantomime.

As a follow-up to the arrangement given here, students might substitute unpitched percussion to each of the parts of the song and substitute the text for the percussion sound (For example, the word *hakova* could be replaced with a drum sound).

Finally, comparing the music for the Hebrew version of this song to an English one (many versions exist) can help children hear how language affects melody: how the three-syllable *lakova* is set differently than the two-syllable "my hat," for example.

לַכּוֹבַע שֶׁלִי שָׁלֹשׁ פִּנוֹת שָׁלֹשׁ פִּנוֹת לַכּוֹבַע שֶׁלִי
וְעִם לֹא הָיוּ לוֹ שָׁלֹשׁ פִּנוֹת לֹא הָיָה זֶה הַכּוֹבַע שֶׁלִי

Lakova Sheli

Traditional/Israeli

Voice: La - ko -va she -li   sha -losh pi -not   sha -losh pi -not__   la - ko -va she - li.   V'-

im lo ha -yu -lo sha -losh   pi -not,   lo   ha -ya -zeh ha - ko -va she - li.

Heiveinu Shalom Aleichem—Teaching Suggestions

About the text

Heiveinu Shalom Aleichem says "we bring peace to all of you." A song to be sung throughout the year, it is often heard at festive occasions both in and out of the synagogue. *Shalom* means "peace," "hello," or "goodbye."

About the arrangement

This is a dance melody and should be performed with energy and spirit. Introduce the song through imitation and echoed response.

To prepare students for the I-IV-V harmony, invite students to follow simple sound gestures (body percussion) as follows:

From this pattern, the class could transfer the body percussion to instruments, patchen becoming "D," snapping to "A," and clapping to "G."

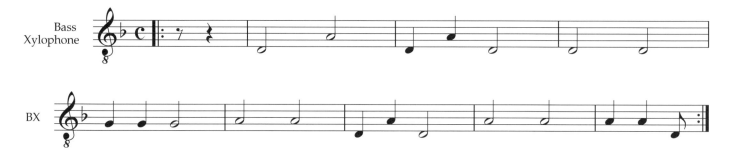

Add other instruments as indicated in the score to help students get into the dance-like spirit of the song. Improvised unpitched percussion parts, based on those in the score, should be encouraged.

Since this is a dance melody, teachers should be encouraged to explore movement when performing. Students might develop a simple dance that includes moving in a circle as in the traditional *Hora*. For longer dances, this might be paired as part of a medley of melodies such as those included in this collection.

הֲבֵאנוּ שָׁלוֹם עֲלֵיכֶם

Heiveinu Shalom Aleichem

Traditional/Israeli

Lo Yisa Goi—Teaching Suggestions

About the text

Lo Yisa Goi, from the book of Isaiah, asks for peace and harmony in the world. An English translation of this is, "Every man by his vine and fig tree shall live in peace and unafraid. They shall turn their swords into plowshares, and nations shall learn war no more." As with many texts from the Jewish tradition, this is only one of many melodies associated with these words. This song is sung throughout the year.

About the arrangement

This canon is a dance melody and is performed at a lively tempo. Introduce the song through echoed imitation. Since the text is the same in both "A" and "B" sections, students should practice the pronunciation of the words carefully.

   Introduce the bass xylophone part by modeling the outline using body percussion (sound gestures) while teaching the song.

   From this, transfer the pattern to barred percussion, as indicated in the score.

   Invite students to discover the scalar pattern on the glockenspiel, which occurs at key parts of the phrase.

   Invite students to learn an unpitched percussion part such as the one in this arrangement. Encourage them to improvise new parts to reflect the class' ideas and abilities.

   A simple movement accompaniment might be added to this piece.

לֹא יִשָּׂא גוֹי אֶל גּוֹי חֶרֶב, לֹא יִלְמְדוּ עוֹד מִלְחָמָה.

Lo Yisa Goi

Music: Shalom Altman
Text: Isaiah 2:4
Canon

Sim Shalom—Teaching Suggestions

About the text

Sim Shalom declares, "Grant peace and happiness, blessing and mercy to all Israel, your people." While the text and setting of this song are sacred, it is sung throughout the year and can be used in non-sacred settings as a song of peace and brotherhood.

About the arrangement

This melody is sung with energy and at a lively tempo. First, the teacher might echo phrases to learn the Hebrew text and melody, noting the repeated phrases of the tune. The first phrase includes Hebrew text but could be sung on a neutral syllable.

Prepare the bass xylophone part by clapping this rhythm while singing.

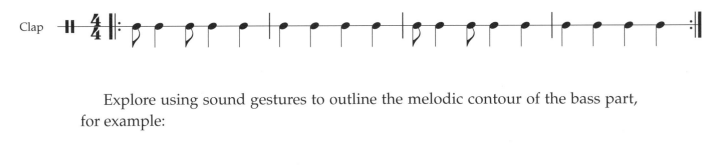

Explore using sound gestures to outline the melodic contour of the bass part, for example:

Then transfer this to barred percussion, as suggested in the score.

Explore the other barred percussion parts similarly, exploring and improvising rhythms in the accompaniment and then transferring these patterns to the instruments. The glockenspiel's countermelody might be played on recorder, flute, or violin.

Encourage students to explore the drum part as written or to improvise patterns based on ideas in the arrangement. In the hand drum part, stems down imply an accented down stroke feel while rhythms with stems up are lighter up stroke patterns.

Since the song has a different accompaniment for each phrase, one group could learn the accompaniment to the first half of the song and another group might learn the second half of the arrangement. The song could be sung *a cappella*.

Sim Shalom lends itself to movement explorations such as a simple dance with two sections.

שִׂים שָׁלוֹם, טוֹבָה וּבְרָכָה.

Sim Shalom

Traditional/Israeli

la la, la Ya la la la la la la la la,

Ya la la la la la la la la, ya la la, ya__ la la.

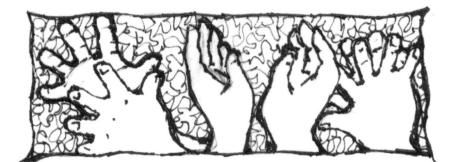

V'David Y'feih Einayim—Teaching Suggestions

About the text

This is a traditional Israeli song about King David (pronounced *Dah-veed* in Hebrew). This song notes that, "David has beautiful eyes (*y'feih einayim*). He tends to his flock in the garden of roses (*shoshanim*)… David conquered tens of thousands; the son of Jesse lives." The text is secular and can be used at any time of year.

About the arrangement

The teacher can present the melody through echoed imitation. To start, this song could be sung on a neutral syllable such as "lai." The first part of this modal melody begins with a simple bordun accompaniment. While learning the melody, invite students to see and hear the bass xylophone part for the first section of the song; then invite students to perform the rhythm of the bass part on their laps. Transfer this simple accompaniment to the instrument.

The second half of the song has a melodic bass line that could be simplified as follows.

From this, more notes could be added, resulting in the part indicated in the score.

Finally, students can add the color parts to the performance. The alto xylophone and glockenspiel parts fall at the end of each motif. Explore the arrangement and improvise new patterns and accompaniments to this dance melody based on the ideas and abilities of the students.

V'David is often associated with specific choreography, but it is appropriate for students to create their own dance to this melody too. Begin with simple dance patterns and explore ways to show the two sections of the melody through movement. For example, in section "A," students could explore locomotor movement, walking in and out of a circle, followed by a non-locomotor section "B," clapping to the beat while standing in place. The original choreography for this dance can be found in many general music sources.

וְדָוִד יְפֵה עֵינַיִם ,הוּא רוֹעֶה בַּשׁוֹשַׁנִים
הִכָּה שָׁאוּל בַּאֲלָפָיו וְדָוִד בְּרִבְבוֹתָיו .בֶּן יִשַׁי חַי וְקַיָּם.

V'David Y'feih Einayim

Traditional/Israeli
Text: I Samuel 18:7

Zum Gali Gali—Teaching suggestions

About the text

Zum Gali Gali is a traditional song from the pioneer days of Israel, before statehood in 1948. The text declares, "The pioneer is made for work, and work is made for the pioneer." The song's rhythmic cadence evokes the monotony of manual labor, similar in style to American labor songs such as "John Henry." One can imagine hammers being struck in unison on every "*zum*."

About the arrangement

The teacher might present the song through rote learning and echoing. Once learned, students can be invited to sing *Zum Gali* using the first two measures as a vocal ostinato. Children might also clap on the word "*Zum*" for added emphasis in the singing of the song and add energy to their performance.

In addition to singing, students might create a simple dance, perhaps moving to the right in the "A" section and left in the "B" section.

זוּם גַּלִי גַּלִי גַּלִי, זוּם גַּלִי גַּלִי גַּלִי.
הֶחָלוּץ לְמַעַן עֲבוֹדָה, עֲבוֹדָה לְמַעַן הֶחָלוּץ.

Zum Gali Gali

Traditional/Israeli

Zum ga-li ga-li ga-li zum ga-li ga-li. Zum - ga-li ga-li ga-li

zum ga-li ga-li. He-cha - lutz l' maan a-vo-dah a - vo-

dah l' - maan he-cha - lutz he-cha - lutz.

D.C. al Fine

S'vivon—Teaching suggestions

About the text

While most Americans call it a *dreydl*, the word *s'vivon* is the Hebrew word for the four-sided top used during the holiday of *Chanukah*. The text echoes the movement of the top, declaring, "*s'vivon* spin, spin, spin." The second half of the song talks of the "*chag*" or holiday that is "*tov*" (good). "*Nes gadol haya sham*" means "A great miracle happened there." These four words correspond to the four sides of the *s'vivon*. The text imitates the idea of the spinning top, first saying that the "holiday is a time of joy where a great miracle happened" followed by the same statement reversed: "a great miracle happened during this joyous holiday."

About the arrangement

The teacher might begin to teach the song by introducing the text rhythmically and then presenting the melody through echoed imitation. As children learn the first part of the song, students could be shown the shifting harmony in the bass xylophone. Invite children to imitate this pattern on their laps and then transfer this to barred percussion. The glockenspiel articulates the phrase and might be added next. This first section can be sung in a two-part canon at one measure.

The second half of the song might be sung *a cappella* or with the given accompaniment. Introduce the contour of the scalar bass part. Scarves or large non-locomotor movements could be used to show the bass line.

Finally, the syncopated tambourine part can be simplified or improvised to add flair to the arrangement. Invite students to add more unpitched percussion parts.

Moving to this song is encouraged. Younger children will enjoy simply spinning like tops as they sing; older students can invent movements with more sophistication. It is also common to sing the song several times, speeding up and slowing down, to imitate the spinning of a top.

How to play *S'vivon* (dreydl).

Everyone places a candy or penny in the circle before the top spins. Each person takes a turn spinning the top. The spinner will follow these rules:

Hebrew letter	Transliteration	Corresponding Hebrew Word	Translation	Action
נ	*Nun*	*Nes*	Miracle	Pass/do nothing
ג	*Gimel*	*Gadol*	Great	Take all
ה	*Hey*	*Hayah*	Happened	Take half
ש	*Shin*	*Sham*	Here	Put one (candy) in

S'vivon

Music: Wolli Kaelter
Text: M. Kipnis

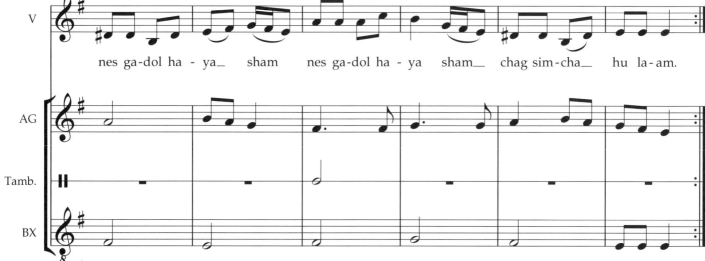

סְבִיבוֹן, סֹב, סֹב, סֹב,
חֲנֻכָּה הוּא חַג טוֹב.
חֲנֻכָּה הוּא חַג טוֹב.
סְבִיבוֹן, סֹב, סֹב, סֹב.

חַג שִׂמְחָה הוּא לָעָם.
נֵס גָּדוֹל הָיָה שָׁם.
נֵס גָּדוֹל הָיָה שָׁם.
חַג שִׂמְחָה הוּא לָעָם.

Nigun—Teaching Suggestions

About the text

This *nigun* is one of the thousands of songs without words (pl. *nigunim*) from the European Jewish musical tradition. This tune is meant to lift the performer to joyous singing, dancing, and celebrating. *Nigunim* originate from a tradition of improvised melodic invention. Teachers should encourage their students to embellish or simplify the tune as they become more familiar with the motifs. It can be performed any time of the year.

About the arrangement

Explore the melody through echoed imitation. Encourage students to identify the two sections of the *nigun*. The first half of section "A" begins with syncopation and ends in a scalar flourish. In this arrangement, a simple bordun accompaniment complements the melody.

The second part of the *nigun* begins with sixteenth note patterns. Explore the rhythmic motifs of the "B" section vocally or on barred percussion. Similar to the "A" melody, the "B" section has a scalar ending.

The accompaniment pattern for the "B" section is melodic. The teacher might present a visual of this bass melody to students and it could also be performed vocally, by a bass recorder, or by string bass. Students might develop a simplified version of the melody and accompaniment.

Other parts might be introduced through sound gestures, echoing, and visuals. If played more than once, invite students to re-orchestrate the arrangement. For example, the group might first sing the melody and then play it on barred instruments. The recorder part might be played on glockenspiel or flute. Embellish the melody based on the basic structure of the tune.

Unpitched percussion parts are suggestions and can be adapted based on student input and ability. In the score, stems down imply an accented stroke while rhythms with stems up are unaccented up stroke patterns.

Nigun

Traditional/Yiddish

Bim Bom—Teaching Suggestions

About the text
Bim Bom is to be performed with energy and spirit. It is one of the thousands of *nigunim* that originate from the European Jewish musical tradition. *Bim Bom* is sung and danced throughout the year. Since the text has no meaning, students may change syllables to make them more singable (*bidi* rather than *biri*, for example).

About the arrangement
Explore the melody using echoed imitation. As children become familiar with the melody, the first half of the bass part can be introduced using the following body percussion (sound gesture) pattern.

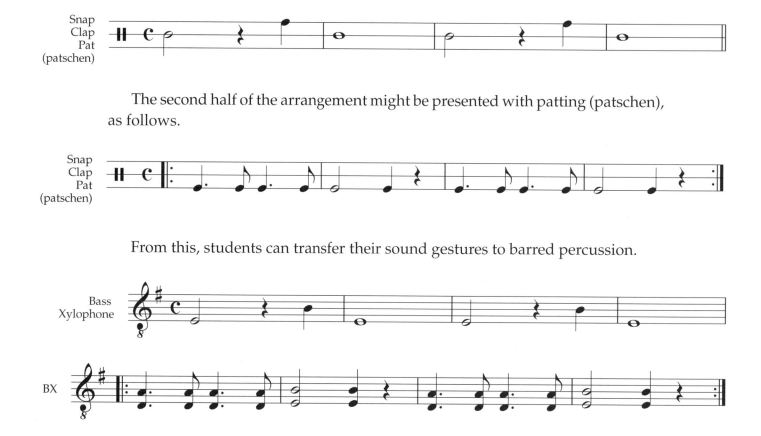

The second half of the arrangement might be presented with patting (patschen), as follows.

From this, students can transfer their sound gestures to barred percussion.

The remainder of the arrangement complements the bass xylophone part and can be taught after the song and bass parts are learned. Invite students to develop or simplify the ideas in the score based on their experience and abilities.

Typically the song is sung with an accelerando and melodic embellishment at each repetition. As a variation, the melody might be played on recorder. Similarly, the soprano recorder part in the score could be played by another melody instrument, such as glockenspiel. Harmonic instruments such as guitar might be added. Improvised interludes after playing the basic melody might be explored when performing this *nigun*.

Explore the unpitched percussion part based on the ideas and abilities of students. In the hand drum part, notes with stems down imply an accented down stroke. Notes with stems up are unaccented up strokes. When playing Middle Eastern doumbek, striking the center or edge of the drum creates different timbres for the instrument. Other unpitched percussion could be added to the arrangement.

A simple choreography might be developed when performing this song.

Bim Bom

Traditional/Yiddish

Haida—Teaching Suggestions

About the text

This *nigun*, or song without words, is to be performed with energy and spirit. *Haida* is one of thousands of *nigunim* extant throughout the European Jewish musical tradition. Freed from remembering text, it was thought, allowed the soul to celebrate the pure joy of the music. Embellishing or simplifying the basic melody is part of the *nigun* tradition.

About the arrangement

Haida can be performed in canon. The teacher might begin to teach the melody using echoed imitation.

While the melody is being learned, students might also be shown the bass part as a simple accompaniment.

After mastering this basic outline of the harmony, additional syncopations and passing tones might be added, as indicated in the score.

Additional parts of the arrangement could then be added through body percussion accompaniments (sound gestures), through rote learning, or through the use of visuals. Melodic variations and embellishments based on the basic structure of *Haida* might be improvised and played after performing the basic melody.

As a movement accompaniment, teachers can encourage their students to create a two-part choreography to the melody. For instance, in the first phrase, students might walk to the left or perform a grapevine step and in the second phrase dance in and out of a circle or simply walk to the right. This could then be performed as a vocal canon with this movement accompaniment.

Haida

Traditional/
Yiddish Canon

Hai - da hai - da   hai - di dee dai da   hai - da   hai - da hai - da

Hai - da   hai - di dee di da   hai - da   hai - da hai - da

Debka Hora—Teaching Suggestions

About the text

A *debka* is a dance genre, much like a *hora, freilach* or other Jewish dance forms. It is a "*nigun*" or song without words. This joyous dance tune should be performed with energy and spirit.

About the arrangement

The melody might be taught as an instrumental piece or on a neutral syllable such as "lai." Invite students to learn the basic motives as the basic "kernels" of the melody, as follows:

Explore the motives in various two-measure combinations. Finally, echo three-measure combinations of motives outlining the actual melody. Perform this simplified melody vocally or instrumentally.

Add more notes from the actual song to each motive. Here is one possibility.

Finally, add the other passing tones as found in the actual song so that the complete melody has been learned.

Improvise the unpitched percussion part, using the score as a template. In the drum part, notes with stems down imply an accented down stroke. Notes with stems up are unaccented up strokes.

Once learned instrumentally or vocally, create a simple choreography to the melody, outlining the two phrases of the tune.

Debka Hora

Traditional/Israeli
Canon

Lai lai lai lai lai lai lai lai.
Lai lai lai lai lai lai lai lai.

lai lai lai lai lai lai lai lai lai.
Lai lai lai lai lai lai lai lai lai.

Hashiveinu—Teaching Suggestions

About the text

This lyrical melody is sung as a three-part canon. The text, from the Jewish liturgy, asks God to "help us to return to you O Lord; then truly shall we return. Renew our days as in the past." Obviously sacred in content, *Hashivienu* is a prayer for the community to come together.

About the arrangement

This plaintive melody is sung reverently. To begin, students should explore each phrase of the melody aurally, emphasizing the musical line of each entrance. This might be sung *a cappella*.

The accompaniment, which outlines the harmonic structure of the canon, might be taught using visuals and solfege. Alternatively, the accompaniment might be sung on a neutral syllable as a fourth part to the canon. Alter the orchestration to the accompaniment by using a string bass rather than a barred instrument.

Hashiveinu

Traditional/Israeli
Text: Lamentations 5:21
Canon

הֲשִׁיבֵנוּ ,יְיָ ,אֵלֶיךָ וְנָשׁוּבָה ;חַדֵּשׁ יָמֵינוּ כְּקֶדֶם.

Hinei Mah Tov—Teaching Suggestions

About the text

There are many different melodies to *Hinei Mah Tov*, but this is one of the most well known. The message is universal: "how good it is for people to live together as brothers." The text and melody may be sung any time of the year, but this version is often heard in synagogues during times of prayer.

About the arrangement

Introduce the canon on a neutral syllable through rote echoing. While doing this, invite students to notice the repetition of the melody.

The bass accompaniment is an elemental ostinato outlining I-V harmony in minor. This might be taught using body percussion (sound gestures) as follows:

Once learned through body percussion, students should be encouraged to transfer this to the two notes in the accompaniment. The alto part in the arrangement complements the bass part and can be presented in context to the bass line as filling in the weak beats in measures 1, 2, and 4. The teacher might begin with body percussion explorations to show the relationship between these parts, as follows:

The other parts can be introduced by highlighting the end of each phrase in the canon. Develop these ideas with children, adding unpitched percussion and more complex accompaniment patterns based on the ideas posed by students.

One might perform the piece as follows:

- Introduction by the Orff ensemble
- Unison singing with accompaniment
- Two part canon with accompaniment
- Two part canon *a cappella*
- Unison singing with accompaniment

Hinei Mah Tov

Traditional/Israeli
Text: Psalm 133:1
Canon

הִנֵּה מַה־טּוֹב וּמַה־נָּעִים שֶׁבֶת אַחִים גַּם יָחַד

Havah Nashirah—Teaching Suggestions

About the text

The melody of *Havah Nashirah* is attributed to Joseph Haydn. The song asks the singer to sing (*shir*) a song of joy and rejoice (*hallelujah*). The piece can be sung any time of the year.

About the arrangement

The students will enjoy learning this three-part canon *a cappella* first. Children can echo each phrase while moving to show the contour of the melody. Invite students to learn the accompaniment either by rote or using musical notation:

This bass line might be performed on other instruments such as bass recorders or a string bass.

Invite students to use the harmonic pattern above as an introduction when performing this canon. A possible performance form would be as follows.

- Introduction by the bass
- Unison with accompaniment
- Three part canon
- Coda by the bass

Havah Nashirah

Canon
adapted from
Joseph Haydn

הָבָה נָשִׁירָה שִׁיר הַלְּלוּיָה

Hodu Ladonai—Teaching Suggestions

About the text

Hodu Ladonai is a beautiful canon. This sacred text from Psalm 118:4 simply states, "give thanks to God."

About the arrangement

The use of melodic sequence in this canon makes it an easy melody to learn. Teachers can present the melody through rote echoing or reading. Students might explore the opening phrase by showing the contour of the melody in motion, using hands or scarves. While the text is simple, singing on a neutral syllable such as "lai" or humming this melody in canon is an inspiring experience. This canon is beautiful when sung *a cappella*. The accompaniment outlines the harmony of the melody.

Teachers or students should be encouraged to create alternate texts that speak of peace, brotherhood, and fellowship to this melody, especially for settings where mention of God is not appropriate. *Hodu L'Adonai* might be used both as a canon or vocal warm up for more advanced singers.

Hodu Ladonai

Traditional
Text: Psalm 118: 1-4
Canon

הוֹדוּ לַיָי.

Shalom Chaveirim—Teaching Suggestions

About the text

"*Shalom*" is the Hebrew word for "peace," "hello" and "goodbye," as in "peace be with you." *Chaveirim* is the Hebrew word for "friends." *L'hitraot* means "until we meet again."

This song is sung throughout the year and asks for peace between all people. A singable English text might be, "Hello my good friends, hello my good friends, hello, hello. 'Til we meet again, 'til we meet again, *Shalom, Shalom*."

About the arrangement

This canon creates beautiful *a capella* harmonies. Once mastered vocally, the teacher might use body percussion (sound gestures) to show the half note pulse as follows:

Snap (r & l hand)
Clap
Pat (patschen)
(r & l hand)

From these sound gestures, the students can transfer this to barred percussion instruments, as indicated in the score. This sparse accompaniment can be a challenge to students who must wait their turn before the next set of players complete the instrumental pattern.

Add movement, possibly outlining the melody's contour using locomotor or non-locomotor movement. Scarves might be used to show this. Such choreographed movement might be used in a performance to visually represent the canon.

Shalom Chaveirim

Traditional/Israeli
Canon

שָׁלוֹם חֲבֵרִים, שָׁלוֹם חֲבֵרִם, שָׁלוֹם שָׁלוֹם
לְהִתְרָאוֹת לְהִתְרָאוֹת, שָׁלוֹם שָׁלוֹם.

Orff-Schulwerk American Edition

MAIN VOLUMES

Music for Children 1	Pre-School	SMC 12
Music for Children 2	Primary	SMC 6
Music for Children 3	Upper Elementary	SMC 8

SUPPLEMENTARY PUBLICATIONS

AFRICAN SONGS FOR SCHOOL AND COMMUNITY
(Robert Kwami)   SMC 551
A selection of 12 songs including traditional material and original compositions by the author.

THE ANCIENT FACE OF NIGHT (Gerald Dyck)   SMC 553
A collection of original songs and instrumental pieces for SATB chorus and Orff instruments. The cycle of songs has both astronomical and musical influences. (Chorus Part: SMC 553-01)

ANIMAL CRACKER SUITE AND OTHER POEMS
(Deborah A. Imiolo-Schriver)   SMC 561
A set of four original poems arranged for speech chorus, body percussion and percussion ensemble. Twenty-one additional original poems are included for teachers and students to make their own musical settings.

ALL AROUND THE BUTTERCUP (Ruth Boshkoff)   SMC 24
These folk song arrangements are organized progressively, each new note being introduced separately.

CHIPMUNKS, CICADAS AND OWLS (Natalie Sarrazin)   SMC 552
Twelve native American children's songs from different regions.

CIRCUS RONDO (Donald Slagel)   SMC 73
A stylized circus presentation using music, movement, speech and improvisational technique, for various Orff instruments, recorders and voices.

CROCODILE AND OTHER POEMS (Ruth Pollock Hamm)   SMC 15
A collection of verses for use as choral speech within the elementary school. Included are ideas for movement, instrumental accompaniments, and proposals for related art, drama and listening activities.

DANCING SONGS (Phillip Rhodes)   SMC 35
A song cycle for voices and Orff instruments. The contemporary harmonies create a dramatic and sophisticated experience for upper elementary/middle school grades.

DE COLORES (Virginia Ebinger)   SMC 20
Folklore from the Hispanic tradition for voices, recorders and classroom percussion.

DISCOVERING KEETMAN (Jane Frazee)   SMC 547
Rhythmic exercises and pieces for xylophone by Gunild Keetman. Selected and introduced by Jane Frazee.

DOCUM DAY (Donald Slagel)   SMC 18
An olio of songs from England, Hungary, Ireland, Jamaica, the Middle East, Newfoundland, Nova Scotia, the USA. For voices, recorders and classroom percussion.

EIGHT MINIATURES (Hermann Regner)   SMC 14
Ensemble pieces for advanced players of recorders and Orff instruments which lead directly from elementary 'Music for Children'; to chamber music for recorders.

ELEMENTAL RECORDER PLAYING
(Gunild Keetman and Minna Ronnefeld) Translation by Mary Shamrock
Teacher's Book   SMC 558
Based on the fundamental principles of Orff-Schulwerk, this book can be used as a foundation text in an elementary music program that includes use of the recorder. It can also be employed in teaching situations that concentrate primarily upon recorder but in which ensemble playing, improvisation and singing also play an essential role.
Student's Book   SMC 559
Includes a variety of songs, pieces, improvisation exercises, canons, duets, rondos and texts to use for making rhythms and melodies.
Student's Workbook   SMC 560
Contains exercises and games for doing at home and during the music lesson. Integrated with work in the Student's Book.

FENCE POSTS AND OTHER POEMS (Ruth Pollock Hamm) SMC 31
Texts for melodies, 'Sound Envelopes', movement and composition written by children, selected poets and the editor. Material for creative melody making and improvisation (including jazz).

FOUR PSALM SETTINGS (Sue Ellen Page)   SMC 30
For treble voices (unison and two-part) and Orff instruments.

HAVE YOU ANY WOOL? THREE BAGS FULL! (Richard Gill) SMC 29
17 traditional rhymes for voices and Orff instruments. Speech exercises, elaborate settings for Orff instruments using nursery rhymes to show how to play with texts.

HELLO CHILDREN (Shirley Salmon)   SMC 572
A collection of songs and related activities for children aged 4–9

I'VE GOT A SONG IN BALTIMORE   SMC574
Folk Songs of North America and the British Isles

KUKURÍKU (Miriam Samuelson)   SMC 57
Traditional Hebrew songs and dances (including Hava Nagila) arranged for voices, recorders and Orff instruments. Instructions (with diagrams) are given for the dances.

THE MAGIC FOREST (Lynn Johnson)   SMC 16
Sequenced, early childhood, music-lesson plans based on the Orff-Schulwerk approach.

PIECES AND PROCESSES (Steven Calantropio)   SMC 569
This collection of original songs, exercises, instrumental pieces, and arrangements provides fresh examples of elemental music. Along with each piece is a detailed teaching procedure designed to give music educators a collection of instructional techniques.

THE QUANGLE WANGLE'S HAT (Sara Newberry)   SMC 32
Edward Lear's delightful poem set for speaker(s), recorders and Orff instruments (with movement and dance improvisation).

¡QUIEN CANTA SU MAL ESPANTA!
Songs, Games and Dances from Latin America
(Sofia Lopez-Ibor and Verena Maschat)   SMC 568
This book presents a rich and varied selection of material from an immense geographical area, combining local traditions with foreign influences to engage and inspire teachers and students. The DVD includes demonstrations of the dances for presentation in the classroom.

THE RACCOON PHILOSOPHER
(Danai Gagne-Apostolidou and Judith Thomas-Solomon) SMC 566
A drama in mixed meters for upper elementary grades with preparatory activities for singing, moving, playing recorder, Orff instruments and creating. The Raccoon Philosopher was inspired by thoughts on virtue by Martin Buber. As we learn from the raccoon, so we learn from the children: to be merry for no particular reason, to never for a moment be idle, and to express our needs vigorously.

RECORDERS WITH ORFF ENSEMBLE (Isabel McNeill Carley) SMC 25-27
Three books designed to fill a need for a repertoire (pentatonic and diatonic) for beginning and intermediate recorder players. Most of the pieces are intended to be both played and danced and simple accompaniments are provided.

RINGAROUND, SINGAROUND (Ruth Boshkoff)   SMC 33
Games, rhymes and folksongs for the early elementary grades, arranged in sequential order according to concepts.

ROUND THE CORNER AND AWAY WE GO (David J. Gonzol) SMC 567
This folk song collection provides models of arrangements to be taught using Orff-Schulwerk processes. The accompanying teaching suggestions give examples of how to break down instrumental parts and sequence the presentation of them developmentally.

RRRRRO
(Polyxene Mathéy and Angelika Panagopoulos-Slavik) SMC 79
Poetry, music and dance from Greece with Greek texts adapted for rhythmic reciting by groups accompanied by percussion and other instruments.

A SEASONAL KALEIDOSCOPE
(Joyce Coffey, Danai Gagne, Laura Koulish)   SMC 55
Original songs, poetry and stories with Orff instruments for children. Bound by a theme of seasonal changes and intended for classroom and music teachers.

SIMPLY SUNG (Mary Goetze)   SMC 23
Folk songs arranged in three parts for young singers. They include American folk songs, spirituals and Hebrew melodies.

SKETCHES IN STYLE (Carol Richards and Neil Aubrey) SMC 19
Arrangements for classroom music. For voices, recorders and classroom percussion.

SOMETHING TOLD THE WILD GEESE (Craig Earley)   SMC 21
A collection of folksongs for unison treble voices, barred and small percussion instruments, and recorders (soprano and alto).

STREET GAMES (Gloria Fuoco-Lawson)   SMC 17
Instrumental arrangements of rhythmical hand jives based on traditional American street games.

TALES TO TELL, TALES TO PLAY
(Carol Erion and Linda Monssen)   SMC 28
Four folk tales (Indian, African, German and American Indian) retold and arranged for music and movement, with accompaniment for recorders and Orff instruments.

TEN FOLK CAROLS FOR CHRISTMAS FROM THE UNITED STATES
(Jane Frazee)   SMC 22
Settings of Appalachian and unfamiliar carols, arranged for voices, recorders and Orff instruments.

TUNES FOR YOUNG TROUBADOURS (Dianne Ladendecker) SMC 34
Ten songs for children's voices, recorders and Orff ensemble.

WIND SONGS (Phillip Rhodes)   SMC 197
Four songs for unison voices, barred and small percussion instruments.